S/S/Y/K (4)

Stop/Sharpening/Your/Knives (4)

First Published in 2010 by S/S/Y/K and Egg Box Publishing

Cover Design: Benjamin Brett, Tim Cockburn, Sam Riviere
Designed and typset: Sam Riviere and Joe Hales
Printed: MPG Biddles

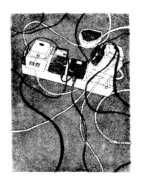

stop/sharpening/your/knives
(4)

Contents

Contents

Illustrations——————————————————————————————

Mollye Miller

Stepping out of the Shade Particles

Without a drop of anything but the drop
full of what
I pull out a grapefruit
splitting its jeweled triangles.
It is a beautiful summary,
noticing things. Opening my pocket
a bit of purple is showing and the orange fish
are swallowing their silk tails
in the middle of their universe.

As I glimpse the streets and step onto a bus
I am always no closer or further.
In this believable garden I am only waking up

Coral, as it Appears

Underneath me the water is my idea –
coral swimming with wireless things.
My idea is not mine but the sea's
floor moving in algebraic stripes
fluffed with daylight fish.
I am the wide eye roaming
the dimensional sea.
The fish part like scaly smoke.
They hover underneath
and bless my stomach
with seaweed waves.
The pomegranate squid
squid home in clear skirts
lifting over rocks
like girls' dresses
by the subway trains.
No one told us what five dollars
a pair of flippers and an iced soda
can get you out of.
That's how for so many
sugary sun minutes
I can lie
on my clear
water orchard
mouth stretched open
with a plastic lip
attached to a long
sky tunnel
and feel gladly I
do not miss my life

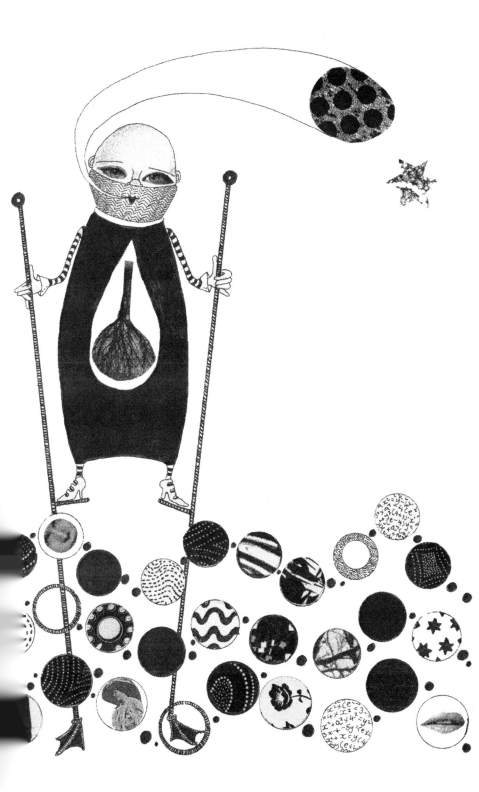

Poem

When whoever brings people together died
we met anyway
and drank blue coffee
from glass mugs on the porch
and listened to each other wrong.
What morning was that, and why
do things end.
Oh, I want you again!

Matthew Gregory

Discovering the Early Humans

We reached what they called Hades with long drills,
breaking the earth's igneous rocks into biscuit.
We were surprised by our lack of mishaps, how shallow
the first reaches of it were. No spitting wells
or spawn, or lakes of blood, nor chambers of white hate.
We lowered our wires, went down one hollow
into another that spanned into a blue panelled room.
At a dresser, the Overseer, reading, with his legs crossed.
You have come with the contract? No, I see
you are not the others, who are to assume my home.
He was an elderly ram, in pointy slippers, a formal tux –
withered, eyes turned in from each dim century.
We were disappointed by his wit, how plausible he was,
how young his face turned when we got up close.

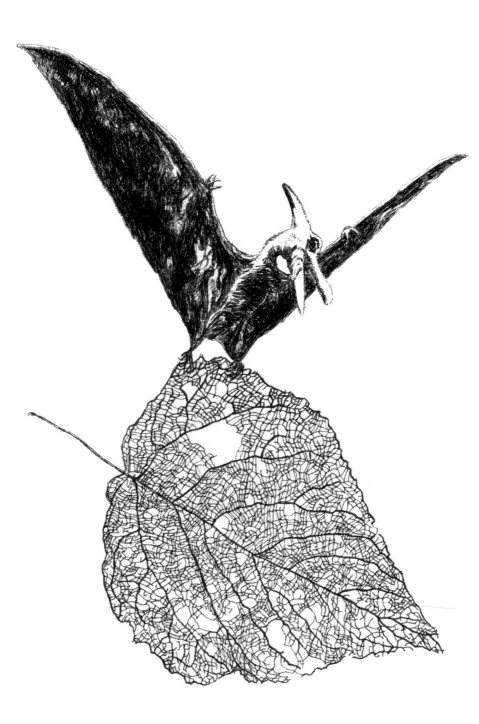

Young Pterodactyl

But we almost didn't notice it, folded into its wings
on the pathway, under rusty leaves.
Don't touch, it will perish if we acknowledge it, I said
but instead you wrapped it in your jumper
and held it in your arms.

We carried it home, a parcel of angles and nerves
and if anyone saw us, I couldn't tell.
The beak was a blunted eggtooth, the rubbery feet
curled inwards the same as a baby's,
but this was new to us.

That night I could think only of its hopelessness;
its eyes, two huge questions in its head.
I built a crate for it to live in; hammering each nail
with a promise to let it go
when the time came.

The next morning I held it, flapping inside my arms
like a dishtowel, while you offered it bits of steak.
It wouldn't eat them and its beak
closed on us for a whole day and night
and we were worried.

Eventually it warmed to us, knuckle-walking on its wings.
Was there anything as childish as this
daft little bone-bird, knock-kneed toy
that we were keeping captive
for our own amusement?

We loved it with our eyes closed; simply, too much,
now it has outgrown us and we are left
clutching after its wake.
Tonight it is enormous as a mood
roosting over our heads.

The Wolves of Novgorod

Andrei and Pavel are discussing the national pest.
Wolves are culpable, in general, Pavel says.
That's the one thing to remember about wolves.

The dachas are lighting up, the pines are thunderous.
Everywhere there are implements and potatoes.
A great man said: *the worse, the better.* It seems worse.

On the stoop with salted pikeperch and borsch
it's time to talk wolf measures, shore up old biases.
To the West the sun slips in the Gulf of Finland.

Wolves will be gathering in the colds of Novgorod.
The foresters are idle, the sheep dogs, indifferent
even though there are no sheep and no sheep dogs

for hundreds of acres in this old beetroot country.
Andrei and Pavel have beards of fleecy pelt,
faces chewed by wind, joints with an arthritic yelp.

They squint into the distant treeline for something
to talk about while their soup congeals and sinks.
There is a scarcity of wolves. Big nothing is howling.

Jon Stone

Boy

I was the Valiant Soldier and so were you.
We took it in turns to be the one slew Boy,
now recalling the teeth that were butcher hooks,

now the pike that was glazed with silver and salt,
the massive, heart-swallowing mouth of Boy,
the tempest of minion and falconet.

Publicans, stable boys, nobles and nobles' wives –
all of them craned for the tale of the killing of Boy.
No one guessed, or if they did, didn't say

that we'd not even sniffed a burning cord of matchlock
and only heard of the dense, cream curls of Boy.
So we won the flesh that seared us more than grapeshot.

Do you feel it too? Throughout the world,
the night is hot and hot with the breath of Boy.
My woman is cold and the punks are especially cold.

Severed by blood, the weapon-proof witches' ally,
Boy, his wounds still running. The gun-dog Boy,
who did catch bullets and spat them, frothing with acid.

I could cross the sea but I could not outrun Boy.
Nuzzling my ribs, his head a bull's head, is Boy,
and when I sleep I sleep in the snarl of Boy.

Trackers, Leash-dogs, and only
a 16 to Heartsease on its back between me and them.
I'm still as a stave but my coat is snapped
by a wind that is mean, white, wine-sharp,
gull-tossing and stink-scattering.
Oh, they are ghastly. One may be Silence,
the other Listlessness but I couldn't be sure.
My breathing dints and undints
a crumpled paper in my breast pocket
as the powerful man arrives on the scene.
He is, I see at once, the most powerful man
in the world. His strides span hamlets.
His skull is a laboratory.
His various facades of character
are a rare and celestial alignment,
and once he has met the dogs in battle
I commando-crawl into the upturned bus,
press against a still-intact pane.
My fingers are filaments of blood.
My watch is a tourniquet.
My wrist is a branch that juts from a car bonnet.
My name label is coming unstuck.
Whoever has won is soon done with the corpse
and turns their attention to me.
Up in flames, I love you. Whips of rain
on the window.

Amy Blakemore

I don't know why you're smiling at all

What if some guy in some suit and tie
should press some button,
      some red button,

and the brick wall you kissed against
goes up in bursts of phosphorescence,

leaving the somnambulists to walk through rubble
nightshirts in tatters, grasping candles,
wiping fallout from their eyes.

What if the worms in the velvet grass,
what if the voices from upstairs,
what if some imp, some red imp

yawning from the burn at the heart of things
should grind two plates together under the sea, what then?

Waves, and death by water,
see your English teacher swept by,
holding her Coleridge high above the waves.
Row for days – see the occasional arch above the water
making an O in the chrome of water.

The raw thoughts and rough fabric
are gone away, with the acts of fierce polyamory,
damp tulips and slim-faced girls from work. What if from the white light,
you hear the voice of God, some guy

who says he's God,
a whisper from the bodybag.

Joe Dunthorne

Fill the blanks

I meet all my girlfriends in the cereal aisle.
They cannot reach the _____.
We agree that it's the delicious flavour
of _____ that starts the day buzzing
like a swarm of _____. 'You are sweet,'
they say, 'and fibrous.' They see the child's seat
of my trolley is empty, which is my cue
to kiss them against the point of sale display.
'I'm _____,' I say, 'but you can call me ____.'
Their eyes are like bowls of _____
with too much milk, and I tell them as much.

They are in my bed. I have all the film tie-in toys
lined up on the mantelpiece. I have full-fat,
semi-skimmed, skimmed, but they just roll over
and keep sleeping. Their name is Phillipa.
Please, wake up.

Margot Douaihy

Late T'ang Dynasty

The market heaves with merchants
selling fruit, jade, polished bone
that once cut flesh.

At dawn, the empress comes
in a black silk robe, doesn't smile
or stay long, lips painted shut
like a tiger's wink in a
lacquer screen.

At dawn, the empress comes
in a black silk robe, fills her basket
and leaves. She seems tired today,
eyes as dark as chestnuts
in the rain.

At dawn, the empress comes
in a black silk robe. Never speaks,
never stays long. A rice boat
floats in. Sun spins into fine
spray over reeds.

That's the empress, I know
it's her. Only the empress
would come at dawn
in a black silk robe
fill her basket
and leave.

Sam Riviere

Rain Delay

'We've discovered Superman's address, and got to the bottom
of the wing-beat rate a beetle needs to stay dry in the rain,
all of which brings to mind the last stand of a certain man
on this very field, what, sixteen years since, is it Greg?
You'll remember Amit's aztec gaze, how he'd play
from a firm back foot, pick his point above your arm,
directing when to kick your wrist and place the pitch, swatting
shots off like dizzy moths – something of the battling mantis
in his awkward height, a bored elegance addressed
by the long circles of his arms. Back home, of course,
he's thought a god, and there always was an uncanniness,
a gift for timing, drawing luck – the rain, like now,
sometimes came with his beckoning, and that feast of charms
rattling about his neck, his slightly eerie victory dance
scuffing dust in geometric shapes, setting a hex
along his crease… The fast bowler from the islands
faced him here in '86, a brutal little ball of a man
with a witchhunter's ardent, direct line. A sad day for sport
when the delivery caught Amit short, bouncing up to touch
his chin, the sweet spot of a perfect uppercut. Down he went,
and never really came around, but you'll remember, Greg,
the swarm of unlikely blood-coloured butterflies
that descended on the pitch, a couple of which can often
be seen this time of year, out there now, batting between the drops.'

The Flaw

There's something black in the green part of your eye.
– Chinatown

'Is this your job, or an obsession?'
Three times, she asked me that question.
I'd smile, keep quiet. Maybe once I lied.
We drove to the orange groves past Echo Park.

You know, husbands look identical, faced
with the evidence, as when weighing the expense.
I unmade men, marriages, my bed.
I always cleaned up after my work.

'I want to know the real you, Jake.'
Why, I'd say, *when you're doing fine with the fake?*
A second before the phone went dead
she gave me the address in Echo Park.

There's one shot left, the struck eye full of blood
and glass. Her stare had found its mark,
meaning my mistake. I lied
once. I drove, I smelled oranges in the dark.

Ben Borek

Bezwład

My cousins (whom I have never met) are visiting for some reason
I will bring them here to the little cottage in the middle of the bypass.

One bright morning in the middle of November, the sky grey and dull,
Night already encroaching, Benjani Benjani B awoke at lunchtime.

My cousins (to whom I hold neither ill-will nor candle) are visiting
For some reason I will cook the table and serve it on itself.

One day at midnight Benjy BB was so hungry he smoked a packet
Of Paramount Finest rolling tobacco. And I mean he smoked the packet.

My cousins are visiting twice, once today and once yesterday.
Yesterday I will take them to the places we didn't make it to today.

One night when the moon was hiding fearfully behind its own shadow
Bennius B Ben threw his cousins out for arriving uninvited, and five
minutes late.

#7

Each night this early summer
After a day of clammy grey
That has leered over us
As if it were an indolent and cataracted eye,
Our open window folds out and receives
A spattering of blunt, wet slashes
From the fractious action painter in the sky.
The garden rises twenty metres high
And Californian Lilac soaks the room.
The neighbour's jaundiced Palm,
At last at home in all this sweaty wind,
Is like a shaggy pineapple
With its bulbous trunk
And shock of unctuous lashes.
Inside, the woodlice have returned.
I free my half-dead arm
And let the blood flow back in thrilling bursts
From underneath the gaudy doll's house
Of your drunken dreaming.
They are benign, these ovoid things
That scutter on the splitting grain
Of moistened, breathing windowpane.
They bear no plague or dirt
And only turn domestic when it's wet.
I watch the frantic vein upon the inside of my wrist
Relieved that it can circulate again.
More shrimp than insect,
You told me this after you had researched
The best way to remove, or kill,
These flecks of garden, overspill
On whitewashed walls, unwashed
For far too long. They feed off dirt.
One other blessing of the warmer nights –
I am allowed to smoke in bed,
So I fumigate the throbbing room.

Charlotte Geater

Moro

There was a bowl on your windowsill.
At first I thought you'd left them there too long
and that oranges could burn, like me last summer,
elbows caught out by the sun.

The flesh was purple. We swapped bruises,
comments on the news. Our bank accounts
were knee-deep in red. You listed locations, and all
I could think (*Belfast*) (*Seattle*) was

this orange is from another country (*Italy*).
Your fingers were too pink for March, each tip
like a thimble. There were charms falling

at your neck, and I, dainty and unsure
leaned over the bin and spat out three seeds
at empty wicker, like gristle, gristle, bone.

Starlings

All birds were starlings.
All music turned to loops,
alarms, caws, my name garbled.
I swear I heard your name,
just once. Starlings got trapped
in our chimney and they never stopped
imitating us. I heard water boil
after all water was sacred.
The country was dead.
I spent hours curled up with you
working out how to make what we had
last. I heard starlings last
making the noise of rain.

Kirsten Irving

No Matter

There's Cat singing here she comes now,
flanking you like Benvolio
and there's an elbow in your side.
You want a banner three feet wide
saying 'The End' and 'Woe'.

Yes Cat, Her love is indeed oh so
fine. She's got his earlobe
nipped between her lips and slides

her finger along his waistband

and it goes right down below
and she tickles Hell and I don't know
if she can see me. I should hide
from her wrists and her street-thief stride
but I stand like a corpse for a crow.

Agnes Lehoczky

I's Notebook

There are a lot of cities I would like not to remember. To talk of them as if they weren't. As if those cities had not existed before. There has to be a hole in the membrane of memory this way. Through which these places can escape into the atmosphere and spill. And refill themselves as memories of no-one and find their home in nowhere. As long as the atmosphere does not eject them. It depends on how many names I could fail to give them. The sunset is not a word, either. Only an incision. Into rocks of greaseproof paper. The sunset is a crater on a photograph. Once upon a time. I didn't want to remember. In a city with a river. This city has not got a name, and the river too, is anonymous. He or she dwelt. A town-dweller, non-significant, who could be I. It is called skinning a white wall. And painting over it again. Depriving space of space. In the end space swells up and all the edges grow together. And there isn't a millimetre of white left on the page to fill with inky hieroglyphs. The strata of all definitions stamped on greaseproof paper. If only I forgot names. I would be back in the same cul-de-sac. What's the point of knowing? What it was I met. I could dwell in here. It would be practical. Names overlap. The topography of memories. Reliefs of the mind, the mini-planet. Each a different colour. The earth's unpeelable skin. They may extend over hundreds of thousands of square kilometres of its surface. And in the end no-one knows. Who I talked about. I could dig down and find the core of it. I could memorise what is *not*. What not to remember. The sunset is not sunrise. The concave not the convex.

Robert Herbert

Excerpt from 'Working Progress'

Our Paris pillow talk
rendered us both champions
of this scatological farce.

Huguenot's feigned sleep
interrupted by laughter. Fart.

This bold curfew a nuisance. A bum
perused drunk thon dark. Said... 'I'm Devil.'

I traded in carpentry.
An Algerian handyman
taught me how
to build bookshelves.

Huguenot flitted & fawned about our halfway house.
We washed like whores
in a kitchenette sink.

I took a Reverend's daughter & a Bostonian student of philosophy
to Parc Floral for a free Free Jazz Fest.

Huguenot, I, & the Swede heard Cali Punks
crunk it in a Bastille divebar, Le Mechanique Ondulatoire.

A Hawaiian pizza gave me bouts of diarrhoea.
'Est ce que vous avez Immodium?'
This pharmacy itched & scratched & coughed & achoo-
ed & this pharmacist's wryish retort
'Bon. Are you passing liquid solids Monsieur?'

'Ca suffis' she said. 'Voila.'

I drank that day dank with beer & cheap wine.

Imagine Huguenot & I streetfighting over dirty dishes & snotrags.

The Swede questioned my sexuality.

'There was this one time when I was with this Mexican guy.
We were in High School, at his house, high.
He had his shirt off. We played *Tekken*.
I looked at him sweat some. Then we fucked. Hard.
His kid brother walked in while I was sucking his cock.
Not since have I had a guy but you are cute.
You know that girl from Yale wants to fuck you.'

I told her about La Coquette. She read aloud Turgenev.
I should have bucked her.
A gruff fattish Texan took me, Huguenot, & the Swede for drinks.
We agreed we thought he was a sex pest.
He took photos of girls asses without asking permission.
He told us he wrote emails to US troops in Iraq
& Afghanistan. To keep them in good spirits.
I should have bucked that girl from Yale.
Huguenot was 'stealing' virginities.

Thon weird voice from Parc Floral.
'We are all monkeys look at all the monkeys!'
He showed me photographs of him shaking hands with world A-listers
His skin was falling off. He gave me his card.

Huguenot & I bathed once a week at Maisie's flat in Le Marais.
He used all her hot water
& I
stank.

Sam Thomas

Hotel Verlaine

Come on let's play a game I lose. I'm left lying here alone
And beauty does not play. The version of this I'm thinking
Of: You blunt the mending needle and booze it up over
My sensible shoes. You gave it all over to some benediction,
Some pope of the after hours and now I'm the foolish virgin
Bride who waits to see her midnight robber beau come home and
Defile her. When you finally stop for nothing I'll make you eggs Cro-
Magnon.

Your escape is starry-eyed but I'll never let you get too far beyond the
Bastards at the gate. And you'd never even know you made it
If you did. How many times did we say this would never happen.

Oh, where I want to live! And how I want to envelop each sigh to you.
I fold them in my sheets. My sheets are full with them already.
If you knew the scent I could arouse in you, you may have come in like a
    lotus.

Instead I lie beside myself. Beside herself. I'll write to you from now
On. If I Bestow it to the sea your ships will enter each gale in fours with
    their
Torn elder masts and planks of beseech. I couldn't watch. I prefer to feel
    you,
I feel you like a hundred empty shells in me. My belly fills with your
Tide and each one chokes contentedly. You leave and they bake in the
    heat
Of madness. I'll care for them and believe them. My beach is as
Wide as your storm.

Alien Pastoral, Montauk N.Y.

Last night, Kristina, the most incandescent
of the Lithuanian food runners decided to
elope with the security guard Ken Bailey.
All along the beach fires blazed orange turning
the sand near cobalt the moon and air were
so clear. Five dollars to Stella's party and the
Sangria and Rolling Rock flowed. Kelly locked
herself in the Corsica with the all the cocaine again
and you lied to Lena and stayed with me.
We all watched as Eamon turned a vat of
Grey Goose into a livid monster blue martini
over at the Shark Shack and were just
starting to groove when Sorana called Lukas
a stupid spic for saying the Romanians were
a bunch of gypsies. You could hear them brawling
in the dirt lot behind the motel till dawn.
By then Liam had grated a raw 'V'
into his forehead body-surfing and everyone blacked out
each unquestionably in love with the other.

Ben Stainton

Esme Carves the Dining Table

She <u>lived</u> that neon necklace & Italian hat.
So I listened, for the morning basin's drip.
Today's Hot Topic added fuel
to already unforgiving weather:

'God is the ideal self', she decided, winding
her watch until the room snapped.
'Everything else depends on its translation;
which artery connects which canal to the sea, etc.'

She said Etc a lot, citing Literature
as a viable excuse for abstaining from sense,
but her best thoughts were always optimistic
failures, leaving marks on plates like soot.

After rubbery coffee, I snatched back
the carving knife; maddened & falsetto.

Hayley Buckland

Owls

The first one whooped its call before breakfast,
the soft arc of a hoot clear cut as we packed.
The second pierced a small heel with gold
and enamel, a speck of blood balled slowly
on the charity badge. The third watched us
swerve off the duel carriageway at seventy –

the juddering of a burst tyre muffled a pulse
in the mouth. As we winced through a skid,
children's singing was shoe-horned to hums
and all babble decelerated in time to the engine.
It swooped past and sat still, erect on the dead
wood and litter, hackles ruffling a coup in the dusk.

Incidental

The guilt is like choking
on talc each morning,

sticking and licking
the air and the throat.

The lines are getting
smaller though,

forming ropes to feel
a path through this

almost pure white,
the wind ringing hollow

through tunnelled ears
still slippery with grease.

There is no soap this big.

Chrissy Williams

Stage Directions for
'The Dog Always Wins'

Act I
[*Rome goes upstairs with a sword, quietly.*
It is still raining. Jules picks up her pen.
A loud knock startles her and she drops it.
The dog enters, grinning. Stage lights fade out.]

Act II
[*Love slowly raises his hammer. All die.*
He looks round, lonely. It is still raining.
Actions are heard whispering at the door.
The dog enters, grinning. Stage lights fade out.]

Act III
[*All the words move offstage and the rain stops.*
The soaked glamour pandas start to tap-dance.
At the back, a screen is slowly revealed.
The dog enters, grinning. Stage lights fade out.]

Tigers

Tarmac. Broken lines are intersecting.
Fog lights on at 15 m.p.h. Dark.
'Did you say you wanted 20?' the way
the shop assistant smelt as he leant in
to ask: a deep lustrous felinity.
(imaginary feathers warn the ground)
Dark. ONLINE BETTING ENTERS THE AGE
OF AQUARIUMS. Fog plumes are streaming down.
Line. Line. Line. Line. The cats' eyes keep time;
red eyes glowering on the left hand side.
(better sorry than safe says the dead bird)
'William Hill are to take internet bets
on goldfish racing. They will take advice
from the most relevant goldfish experts.'
Headlights ignite the fog. *I tawt I taw...*
I think deceleration is the key.
Just keep moving.

Heather Phillipson

Heliocentric Cosmology

Got what?
asked my husband through a mouthful of mashed potato.
I was at home with my husband, eating mashed potato.

Two miniscule but unequal balls of mashed potato
dropped from his mouth onto the mashed potato.

It was like when Galileo dropped balls of the same material
but different masses from the Leaning Tower of Pisa,

except Galileo didn't use his mouth or mashed potato,
and the ground isn't a plate of mashed potato.

I've got it!
I stopped eating mashed potato.

I looked up from the mashed potato.
My husband looked up from the mashed potato.

I've got it!
I slammed my fist into the central, glowing platter of mashed potato.
It was hot, for mashed potato.

Orbs leapt.
They were loose crumbs of unmashed potato.

Some moved towards the mashed potato.
Some moved away from the mashed potato.

I had discovered that the earth goes around the sun.
Of course, Copernicus discovered it first.
But I rediscovered it.

Nathan Hamilton

Malcolm Training

lone Malcolm kicks at shadows in the long evening
the wind busy scribbling him out
his old candles depart a filigree   treelike

he is here with strange gravity building
the landscape is altogether and in bits   alien   sound
bunched rows obscure a field view

quite where is the mark to be far off from
oh where the sleepy buds of spring
a way to say goodbye at this point may be touching

Malcolm Judged

he is a crime of sorts and very anti most things
does not like to joke   instead works hard
is a bad guest virtually made of stealing

he finds in lack of quip a gruel   tends to transgress
always wants to orbit the party with thinking
much as tax worry wrecks a semolina

he is therefore likely to frustrate ordinary banquets
so sentence Malcolm!
Picked for this: a broad panel of twats.

Michael Zelenko

Hover

At family reunions the men poured Cognac for the ladies
And vodka for each other.
I would look up then:
My father's face shrank and his arm swept across the table.
He was reaching to touch someone, or else just
Fanning the table's snowy canvas.

At other times, between friends,
His hand would search for the loneliness of
White wine. It waited for him:
The only bottle left unopened.
The one on which a mother was shown holding a naked child,
Was a favorite; the one in which the father
Was relegated to the spiritual.
He floated over the party like an abandoned astronaut
Or a low flying gull.

But at 22 I remember finishing my beer,
And moving to pour out its dredges.
My father stopped my hand:
'That's still beer,' he said,
Swallowing gracefully.
His eyes swelled and watered
And he plummeted at incredible speeds.

Meghan Purvis

The Birdhouse

A slug lies half-squashed on the front stoop.
The nest is feathered: a collage of overgrown shrubs,
flyers for pizza shops and a slug with its slug-guts
spilling out in a straight line where the bike hit.

The house looks at you one face-side at a time,
the cocked head, the hidden-pupil eye.
The house squats on things, warming them;
a home brewing system, a rust-blocked rifle.
A cat squats and watches, its elbows out.

It has brought you things: the glint of rain
on pavement, a magpie snippet of broken windows.
Here is where the skins of things are spat out.

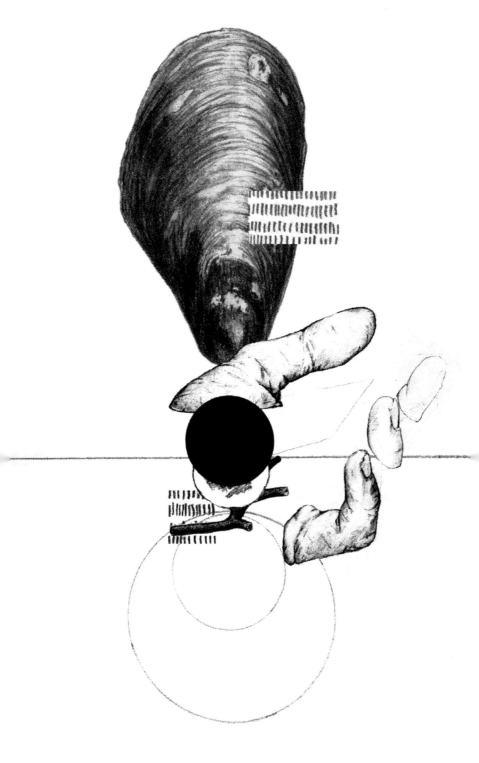

Joe Kennedy

An index of northern defiling brown
under weatherings, tea caps flipping
lid roses making the lea of the crop crowned
with stumps a bower. Brook to byre:
striped she was caught there and striped again
on wide verges trending east.
Every lad sang! Sang in our fat!

I wasn't well. They tanned
by the moor pond, rapped mussel shells:
pink fingers callused on mail, and fat.
The aspect bred and the chat of advance
clipped and gated, waved and was waived –
dispersing, garish cars lent modish closure.
It was all over in the lay-by.

Emily Toder

There was an ellipse in the vineyard
when I woke up
a grainy nervous ellipse wavering
over the tops of the dead harvest
so I went up to it
I had not had any coffee yet
It was knit and its knit texture
startled me as I approached
such a tedious affair to create a thing like this
such handiwork it was major craftsmanship
I felt curious about who had done that
and what they were doing right now
The well-done thing looked jittery
it seemed to be stuck in one of the vines
Normally an ellipse will sway in the wind
and fade
This one was dizzying
I took some of its perimeter in one of my hands
and I took the vine in my other
and I severed them
like you would sever a pizza
The ellipse began its drift
carelessly in the wind it unwove
I stood in the wind with it
until it was gone and
I was alone with my plot
and that weary vine
that was also alive
and troubled
and devout
and floored

I closed my eyes for a while
and when I opened them there was a rectangle
it was multi-colored and nonchalant
kind of ambiguous-looking
That is a postal package said my neighbor
someone loves you
It is a tissue box said my other neighbor
watch it shed its tissues like little kites
It is a toaster oven said a jogging passerby
you should watch out, those things
are dangerous
I looked down at my feet where it was printed
welcome. I looked up at the rectangle
and I felt welcome there too
You will have to sign for it said my neighbor
You will feel better said my other neighbor
They start housefires all the time said the one jogging
they cannot handle most breads
the crumbs at the bottoms of them get gas on them
The rectangle stood steadfast on my lawn
some of its sides began unfolding
maybe from the wind
it unfolded its flaps to me and I went up to it
Take this knife to cut its tape said my neighbor
Take this net to catch its tissues said the other
Be sure it is unplugged said the one jogging
The rectangle was unplugged
I live in a friendly town in which
we all look out for one another
Watch out! my neighbor called
Look at that giant jaw
Oh my god said my other neighbor
And the jogger just screamed
and screamed

There was a hexagon in the floor
of the house I was summering in
a shy pumpernickel hexagon
with nice earth tones to it
in the middle of the summer
I had no one to consult with because
I had been outcast for decades
and had not been around
anyone or a hexagon in a long time
for my family I was dead
it had said You are dead to us
a long time ago
and the community had
supported them and banished me
even from my favorite rock
at the lip of the bridge
I did not know how to act around the hexagon
I was walking funny
always diverting my path
in a way it was the way
I had always behaved
I took a kind of liking to the hexagon
and took turns standing beneath each of its sides
which I could not distinguish
like I had always behaved
I gave the hexagon food and shelter
and it became part of my household
and I gave it chores and looked after it
like it was my own son
Do not betray what we stand for I warned it
Or I will cut you off
and you will be dead to me
that sounded about right
Some time later the thing rotated
and my floor cracked
the boards sprung up splintered
and a chunk of the wall powdered

You have shattered what we stand for
now you are dead to me
I had an itch it said
There was a chopstick of a rumble
the foundation of the house fell in
and a rafter came down sidelong
and destroyed all my figurines
When I came to
the hexagon was holding a compress to me
That was pretty nasty it said
I hope I am not still dead to you
I told it I would make an exception this once
but the thing grew suddenly pale and blue

Jack Underwood

Consequences

I need to tell you that your elbow
fits fully in the nook under my chin,
that I want to put your lovely ear
up to my mouth and sing myself inside.

I'm so used to looking into your eyes,
I forget the names of colours.
I want to bend your knees. Your feet
are extremely well proportioned.

Now say 'avocado' and let me see
your armpit. I am a buffoon for you;
scratch my bright, scabby head.
Lace your shoes as usual.

Dog Walking Backwards

It said if I tried to climb for Christ
I'd only be told to sit and stay.
And as It spoke my veins flushed in,
my body sunk and holy holy,
dog-leg, leg-dog, It traversed
the alley slowly in reverse.

What O why did I not scream,
Its tail checking, out in front,
Its snout face, facing back, eyes
fixed on me? It was miraculous.
I felt my jaw go, my legs
go and then my Hallelujah.

Charlotte Hoare

Autumn –

I have boiled these pears for your branches –
They turn and blink clearly in water
Like skinless hands, hanging reachless.
They seem as white as rock. And stiff and sweet
In their last speaking, when I cut
And they slump hotly like sugar. So have them.
To show I spoke once too –
Held leaves like something growing, like a voice.

Callan Davies

Lighting Out for the Territories

Too still. The milk's goin warm
an Bugs gonna be lame before next week
Uncle says. Uncle says a storm fixing
from somewhere up yonder. Can smell it
in the blind air. Too still it is here.
Can't even hear the river sometimes
or smell it. Can feel it though. Things always
goin missing or getting mixed up means
you know the river here – taking off its hat
and bowing and putting it on calm-like
to us poor folks sat on its banks. Like it don't
got a care in the world. And so it ain't
moving on down alltimes like that. So it ain't.
Aunt's down at the barn collecting eggs and singing
under her breath. Gotta break the air with something she says
not even birdsong about to battle the heat of midday.
No. Too still. Soft and civilise like. I's waiting for the wind.
It's coming – for certain. Uncle says – it's in the air.

Theodore Best

English as a Foreign Language

today
a man stands in a bottom corner
by an equals sign

his arms
are limp black daffodils
blue dots arc from his eyes

yesterday his mouth was a bowl

★

three clouds rise
from a young man's frown

in the last he's on his knees
and a woman with green cheeks
says of course I will exclamation mark

★

there are eleven dashes on the board

we have

s blank r blank n
d blank p
blank t y

under this
a man with x's for eyes
hangs by his neck from a gallows

some of the alphabet watches

★

a man is on the phone

his right foot is in the mouth of a dog

at the left of the board
a woman with a dot for a mouth
has answered a call

a squiggly line connects them

★

a house has a broken window

a woman in the doorway
has one hand on her cheek
and a mouth like a boomerang

at the right of the board
a man with a big bag and a mask
is running

above them

Passive Voice

★

today
the board is covered in fruit

tomorrow it will be vegetables

next week animals the names of meat
cutlery cook cooker the kitchen

bedroom bathroom
living room on Friday

Emily Berry

David

The hand that writes is the executive hand,
says Nurse Glory. We're writing postcards
at the Stazione di Santa Maria Novella.

The other is the bad hand! she warns.
In case I forget I write MY BAD, GLAD HAND
on the back of my left, but the ink runs;

I'm sweating. When we walk the streets
of Europe's cities Nurse Glory's executive hand
keeps hold of my bad because I am untrustworthy.

Sometimes she lets her own bad hand slap me
and then she makes a fist with her good hand
and bites it and looks terribly contrite. In Hamburg

she marched me up and down the Reeperbahn
shouting: *This is what becomes of bad girls!* I'm not
absolutely the most hopeless case she's ever had

on her sainted hands, Nurse Glory says, but mercy,
I'm not far off. *Dear Doctor,* my postcard begins.
My correspondence with the Doctor is strictly

confidential. As a result, I never write to anyone else.
I'm writing to you with my executive hand. Today
we said goodbye to the Duomo and the Ponte Vecchio.

Phew-ee! It's hot, and sad. I miss you. Love, Me.
The picture on the front is of Michelangelo's David,
which Nurse Glory forbade me to see. Like all

mental health professionals, she's obsessed with
genitalia. *P.S.*, I add, *David's ball-sack looks like an
upside-down heart.* My innocence is really incredible.

Dear Boy

Actually it's Tuesday, and I'm taken aback.
   You rang me three times and said *I can explain everything*
into my voicemail. You know perfectly well I believe nothing worthwhile
   is explainable. Dear boy, don't be so literal.
I'm not sure if you were there or not. Did you want to be?
   We can make something up. Perhaps it was you I parasailed with
above the Mediterranean? I think I remember you now; my young love!
   You complained that the harness was hurting your balls.
We had such plans. We were slung between sea and sky. I tangled your legs
   in mine. We were a knot in the grain of the world.
Suddenly the sea was a blunt spur at our heels, remember?

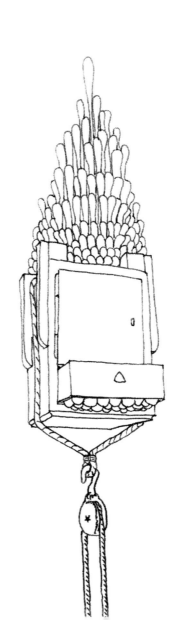

Tim Cockburn

Deco

I love you because you are like love
a flimsy and preposterous thing,
like a deco bedside cabinet
whose gold trim is coming away,
whose quilted sides are yellow and punctured,
but that you buy anyhow,
if only because, among the serious junk,
its cheerful stab at flair seems
a certain defiance, a retort.

Sex and the City

walking to a garage not because
you want anything but because
at home everyone is shoving into each other

staring at a carton of juice
which shows an orange skipping with a cane
and two grapes laughing at the orange

Reminder about the
songs currently in the charts

They mean how beautiful and near she is.
Though now each asks no more than to rest
an elbow on your consciousness
as a tired lane swimmer pauses for breath
at the end of the pool, then pushes away again,
when they do it won't be forever;
they will catch you in some bar or bedroom
and mean how beautiful and near she is.

Appearances in the Bentinck Hotel

Sometimes in going to pick something up,
however casually certain your fingers it is one thing,
looking may show it to be another,
just as sometimes in telling someone you love them,
however casually certain your tongue the words are true,
on the ear they may fall as forced or artificial,
and in saying them you may come to realise you don't,
or not as you thought, and it will seem
a kind of sneakiness on the part of the words,
as it does on the part of my lager, when playing pool
I swig from it and it is not my lager
but your lager top, or even in coming to write a poem,
when it shrugs at you from the page and says,
No poem here, only the bones of one at best,
and those you reject as too deliberate or too cute,
since always it is possible that for forty minutes
exactly my lager is a lager, on my ears on my tongue
to the touch I love you, and this is the Bentinck Hotel.

Biographies

Hannah Bagshaw graduated from University of the Arts London with a degree in Fine Art and has completed an MA in Illustration at Camberwell College of Arts. www.hannahbagshaw.co.uk

Oliver Beavis is an artist and illustrator living and working in East London. His works stem from his surroundings, but also encompass typographic elements and influences. oliverbeavis.tumblr.com

Emily Berry won an Eric Gregory Award in 2008. *Stingray Fevers*, her pamphlet, was published the same year. She is working on her first collection, and co-writing *The Breakfast Bible*, published by Bloomsbury.

Theodore Best studied Psychology at Goldsmith's and Philosophy at King's College London. He is a recent graduate of the MA in Poetry at the UEA.

Amy Blakemore was born in 1991 and was a Foyle Young Poet of the Year twice. She has gone on to have work published in a variety of places, including *Voice Recognition: 21 Poets for the 21st Century*.

Ben Borek lives in South London. *Donjong Heights*, a novel in verse, is published by Egg Box Publishing.

Benjamin Brett studied fine art at the Norwich School of Art and Design, and continues his studio practice in painting and drawing.

Hayley Buckland completed an MA in Creative Writing at the UEA in 2006. She lives in Norwich with her husband and three children.

Tim Cockburn was born in 1985 in Banbury, Oxfordshire, and raised in Nottingham. He is a graduate of the MA in Creative Writing at the UEA. He lives and works in Norwich.

Callan Davies is in his third year at Exeter, where he studies English Literature. He is a former winner of the Foyle Young Poet of the Year.

Grace Denton grew up in Yorkshire. She graduated from the UEA in 2009 and now lives and works in Bristol.
http://gracedenton.tumblr.com/

Richard Dinnis is an artist, illustrator and printmaker. His first book, *A Postcard from The Mountains with The Mountains Tipp-Exed out*, was published in 2008.

Margot Douaihy an instructor of literature at Marywood University. Her poetry has appeared in magazines including *The Poet's Corner*, *Big Bridge*, and *Pittsburgh Post-Gazette*.

Jim Dunn is a designer and illustrator who lives in Norwich.
http://jimmdunn.me

Joe Dunthorne's debut novel *Submarine* has been made in to a film by Warp. His debut poetry pamphlet is published by Faber and Faber. He co-organises a night of literary miscellany, *Homework*, in East London.

Beatie Fox received an MA in Drawing from the University of the Arts, London in 2009 and was awarded the Evelyn Williams Trust Bursary.
beatiefox.blogspot.com

Charlotte Geater is a submissions editor for the online magazine *Pomegranate*. Her first play, *Toffee*, was performed in Oxford in spring 2010.

Matthew Gregory was born in Suffolk in 1984. He studied at the Norwich School of Art and Design and Goldsmiths, University of London. In 2010 he received an Eric Gregory award.

Gawain Godwin studied Critical Fine Art Practice at Brighton University and Fine Art at the Norwich School of Art and Design.

Joseph Hales is a London-based Graphic Designer. He has worked for Tate and on many independent publications. www.josephhales.co.uk

Nathan Hamilton runs Egg Box Publishing. His poetry and criticism have been published in a number of places, including *Poetry London, The Manhattan Review, The Rialto, The Guardian,* and *The Spectator.*

Lisa Handley is an illustrator who lives in Manchester. www.lisahandley.blogspot.com

Fay Elizabeth Heffer was born in 1987. She lives and works in Norwich, and is re-locating to London in January 2011. www.fehillustration.com

Robert Herbert is from Co. Down, Northern Ireland. He is currently studying for a PhD in Poetry at the University of Liverpool. His poems have appeared in *Brand, Gallous, Kritya, Tower Poetry*, and *Poetry Proper.*

Charlotte Hoare grew up in the village of Potterne, Wiltshire. In 2007 she moved to Norwich to study at the UEA. Right now she's learning to teach English Language in Prague.

Peter Holden is an illustrator and printmaker based in South Devon. He recently finished studying at the University of Gloucestershire.

Kirsty Irving co-edits *Fuselit* and Sidekick Books, and is currently putting together her first collection. Her work has appeared in *Polarity, Hand+Star, Mercy* and *Dwang.*

Suki Kalsi is a York-based artist specialising in mixed media, including photography, textiles and collage. Her work appeared in the *Aesthetica Creative Works Annual 2009.*

Joe Kennedy he completed a PhD on 1940s English fiction in 2008 and has subsequently taught at the UEA. He writes for a number of publications including *3AM* and *The Quietus.*

Alice Lee is an illustrator and filmmaker with a degree in Animation from the Norwich School of Art and Design.

Ágnes Lehóczky is a Hungarian-born poet. *Budapest to Babel* is her first English collection . She is a recipient of the Arthur Welton Poetry Award and has been selected as the winner of the Daniil Pashkoff Prize 2010.

Tracey Long is an illustrator. Her work can be found here: www.traceylong.co.uk

Helen Maier lives and studies in London most of the time.

Mollye Miller graduated from The New School in New York City with an MFA in poetry. Her photographs can be found here: www.flikr.com/photos/mollyemiller

Ali Page completed a Fine Art Degree in 2003. Her first solo show took place in December 2008 and she collaborated on the drawing-based exhibition *Blue Tigers* in the summer of 2010.

Heather Phillipson's pamphlet was published by Faber and Faber in 2009. Her poems have appeared widely in magazines and anthologies. She is also an acclaimed artist and filmmaker and exhibits internationally.

Meghan Purvis was born in California and graduated from Oberlin College in 2003. Her work has appeared in *The Rialto*, *The Frogmore Papers*, *Magma*, and *The Comstock Review*.

Sam Riviere received a 2009 Eric Gregory Award, and is currently working towards a PhD at the University of East Anglia. Faber and Faber published his pamphlet this year.

Ben Stainton lives in rural Suffolk. His poems have appeared in *Horizon Review*, *FuseLit* and *Nthposition*. He is currently studying Art History and working on a second book.

Tristan Stevens was born in Montreal. Exhibitions include BaZtille (Netherlands) and OUTPOST Gallery (UK).

Jon Stone is co-creator of cult arts journal *Fuselit* and micro-anthology publishers Sidekick Books. His debut pamphlet *Scarecrows* is out now from Happenstance.

Zoë Taylor has recently been commissioned by Luella Bartley, *AnOther Magazine*, and London Fashion Week's *The Daily*. She's working on a graphic novel. www.zoetaylor.co.uk

Sam Thomas divides her time between Miami, Ireland and England. She is currently finishing the MSt in Creative Writing at Oxford and just starting on a screenplay commission.

Emily Toder is the author of *Brushes With*, a chapbook from Tarpaulin Sky Press. Her translation of Edgar Bayley's short fiction is due out this autumn from Clockroot Books.

Jack Underwood teaches Creative Writing at Goldsmiths College, where he is studying towards a PhD. He won an Eric Gregory Award in 2007, and his pamphlet was published by Faber and Faber in 2009.

Megan Whatley was born in South Africa and moved to England as a teenager. She has an MA in Authorial Illustration in Cornwall and currently lives and works in West Sussex.

Amelia Whitelaw graduated in 2008 from Chelsea College of Art, London. She was awarded a major commission by The Courtauld Institute for the 2008-09 East Wing exhibition *On Time*.

Chrissy Williams has had poems published in *The Rialto*, *Dial 174*, *Orphan Leaf Review*, *Fuselit*, *Rising,* and *South Bank Poetry* She works on the Poetry Library's digital magazine archive.

Michael Zelenko is a writer and freelance editor living in San Francisco, California. His non-fiction writing has appeared in *TheRumpus.net*, *The Reykjavik Grapevine*, and *Where* magazine, among others.

Anthony Zinonos is a Norwich-based artist/illustrator. www.anthonyzinonos.com

S/S/Y/K

This anthology was edited by Emily Berry, Nathan Hamilton, Sam Riviere, and Jack Underwood. The cover art is by Benjamin Brett. The image of the plugs on the title page is by Oliver Beavis. All the illustrations were produced in response to the poems featured in *S/S/Y/K* (4). Invaluable assistance designing this book was provided by Tim Cockburn and Joseph Hales.

S/S/Y/K (5) is open for submissions. If you wish to submit your poems or illustrate for the book see here for more details –
www.stopsharpeningyourknives.co.uk

Thank you for buying this publication.